# Friends Like These

Eden Gruger

© 2023 Eden Gruger
All rights reserved.

Eccentric Girl Press

Print ISBN: 978-1-7398642-4-8
Ebook ISBN: 978-1-7398642-3-1

The right of Eden Gruger to be identified as the author of this work has been asserted by him in accordance with the Copyright, Designs and Patents Act 1988.

All rights reserved, no part of this publication may be reproduced, stored in or introduced into a retrieval system, or transmitted, in any form, or by any means (electronic, mechanical, photocopying, recording or otherwise) without the prior written permission of the publisher. Any person who does any unauthorised act in relation to this publication may be liable to criminal prosecution and civil claims for damages.

Book design by Sarah E. Holroyd (https://sleepingcatbooks.com)

I would like to thank the real-life members of my family, friends, others and the universe, memories of, and about whom have helped inspire this book.

Having said you inspire me, any and all items with a factual basis have either been changed, (re-) invented, altered or included for expressive use (and as a necessary component of the relevant story).

That means that as a fictionalised work, no person or event depicted is to be taken as fact, as they are not. Any offence or displeasure is unintended, and I would be very sorry should you think that my characters are you. Or that events are a factual representation of anything that has happened.

This book is for the friends who have come into my life, and taught me something before they moved on.

And most especially to the friends who have come into my life, and made everything more wonderful just by being there.

# Contents

| | |
|---|---|
| Frenemy vs. The Frully | 1 |
| Pastor Elliot | 7 |
| Childhood friends | 11 |
| Further Education | 17 |
| Radical Restyle | 23 |
| Cold Soup and Amphibians | 30 |
| What is this thing I hear you speak of? | 34 |
| Sounds So Fake It Must Be True | 42 |
| When sharing is bad for you | 48 |
| Strawberry Cervix | 55 |
| Hula Girl | 59 |

# Frenemy vs. The Frully

You may not currently be aware of either of these things, but I can virtually guarantee you have met one, or the other (or both). You may even have one in your life right now.

If at the end of this page you think oh no, this is horribly familiar, prepare yourself to cut those ties. Both real and psychic, because these people don't tend to learn how to value the people in their lives.

Of the two the frenemy is almost preferable, although still not very nice to experience. But at least this is a more honest form of not very nice. A frenemy is the person who you are friendly with, regardless of the fact they have a basic dislike of you.

They may not even be aware of this themselves, it's likely that it comes from some underlying rivalry. Whether that's over wealth, beauty, education, holiday destinations, personality or partners. Generally, you will know them as part of a larger group of friends. Which makes it much easier to avoid being stuck with each other one on one.

Your common or garden Frully while sharing many qualities in common with the frenemy is a much more insidious creature. They are the one you (and probably your partner and family), socialise with.

They are someone whom you probably confide in, and you better believe they store every bit of dirt they hear about you. And that's part of the issue, because they know your secrets, they understand how and where to hit you so that it really hurts, and baby they aren't afraid of doing it.

You will get a little bit of something positive from them, maybe babysitting, or help when you are running late for the school pick up. They could be the person who listens to you cry into your cocktail after a big fight with your other half. Or who nods and agrees with you when you feel your boss is being unreasonable.

That's all part of the lure that keeps you coming back for more. How can they be so kind, and so mean? Because they aren't doing anything from kindness, they are collecting evidence.

Friends Like These

Being a canny baggage, they will remember all the times things go wrong in your life, or you mess up, ready to use to control you.

Whether that's dropping little hints about your 'failings' in front of others to unsettle you, and make you doubt yourself. Or making jokes that hurt. You'll probably tell yourself that you could be being too sensitive, right? I mean, they are your friend…

But as your bully they need you to feel they, (and by implication everyone) see you as lower status than you actually are. Remember this type of bully enjoy pulling people down, if you are already there you aren't of much use to their ego. They'll use all the smiling daggers in their armoury to undermine you. And if they can get close enough, they will influence every choice you make, without you even noticing.

Eventually you will reach the point where you need to defer to them in everything. What you wear, where you go, and the other people you choose to have in your life.

I heard of one Frully who divorced her husband for unreasonable behaviour. Unreasonable in that he objected to her affair. Who worked away on her best friend until she also filed for divorce from her own perfectly acceptable husband. Why would anyone do such a thing you ask?

In the Frully's eyes sharing custody of her children and taking a financial cut in her lifestyle would make her lower in the pecking order. And there was no way she could allow it. She also wanted to guarantee her follower would be available for the new activities she would be involved in. That's why, they are ruthless.

Another friend was getting ready for an evening out at a Frully's house, and once dressed and ready, asked "do I look ok?". The Frully replied "you really don't have to worry..." pausing just long enough for my friend to give a sigh of relief, before finishing, "no-one will be looking at you anyway".

My own Frully listened to me talk about how my not wanting to go out as much socially was causing issues with my partner. And my concerns over his flirting. Then said, "that's out of order, he cannot expect you to be as lively as one of us young ones". I was thirty five, and she was thirty two.

Which is an absolutely horrible Frully move. Putting you down whilst elevating themselves, it's classic.

If when introduced to your new partner they say in front of them, "wow you've done well for yourself," and mean it. This was not a compliment for them, it was a put down for you.

This is good for the Frully in two ways, it keeps you down and shows the new person in your life who's in control, and it's them.

Watch out for someone in your life who listens to you, but who later mentions something painful you have talked about. They might do that in company, or at a time when you are feeling really good about yourself.

When you think about them, you'll eventually notice that they never share any of their bad days. They don't take chances that someone else could make them vulnerable.

Do you have someone who you organise things with, who leaves you to do all the arranging and organising? And who nearer the time drops into conversation the holiday or trip, or whatever they are doing at the exact time you agreed?

They will behave as if you had never had the discussions or made any plans. In their world your time and energy are worthless, and anything you do is just not important in their life. Such a Frully.

If you are kind and caring these people are easy to pick up, and some of us make an unintentional habit of it. But unlike them, we can do it differently. As soon as you set boundaries (however nicely), they will move on. Then you can focus all your love and attention on real friends.

The ones who think you are gorgeous inside and out, trust you to take responsibility for your choices without taking over. And who have time for you whether life is going up or down.

Go on tell me honestly, how many Frenemies or Frullies have you collected?

# Pastor Elliot

Angelica and I used the bus not just for getting from here to there, but also as a great place to people watch. We had been privy to a variety of sights, many of which really shouldn't have happened on public transport.

Including tooth-pick man, who we only noticed when we heard a random clicking noise and turned to see a man using one overly long fingernail, on his left hand to pick his teeth. What a delight.

Then there was hungry bum, a lady with her back to the centre doors who spent the journey trying to adjust something in her butt crack. We guessed a tight thong maybe? she was trying not to be too obvious. Sadly, the angle of our seats gave us a completely uninterrupted view of the anal digging expedition.

And of course, there were all the get-a-rooms, usually (but not always) teenagers. Who seemed to believe they were invisible, either that or their hormones were so rampant they couldn't care less who saw them doing what.

Imagine what people might be doing in the privacy of their own house with no-one watching, and you have the idea.

On this particular trip nobody was doing anything either repulsive or hilarious, so we resorted to reading posters. We were independently moved to point out a colourful advertisement on the wall above us for a chap called Pastor Elliot.

He looked so happy, the energy of his congregation although their image was blurred, practically fizzed out of the poster towards us. The other thing that we noticed was how elaborately dressed they were. We were instantly taken with the idea of being amongst these glamourous worshippers.

I think what amused and impressed us so much, was no-one in our own church ever got dressed up like that. Sunday best being very much an idea rather than an outfit. Even when they were invited to a wedding, they often didn't have this vivacity.

We liked being in the sort of church where people could come in jeans and t-shirt. But we also liked getting dressed up, and Pastor Elliot we immediately saw was offering us this opportunity in abundance.

Pastor Elliot became a byword for everything sparkly, dramatic and red carpet. The rest of the day one of us would pick up something in satin, with ruffles, or both, and say it was nice, but was it Pastor Elliot nice? To which almost everything got a solid no, before being returned to the rail.

That was until we found a designer outlet store, with ball gowns and cocktail dresses and everything in between. With enough rhinestones to induce a migraine, and sequins to bring on an epileptic fit.

We held these amazing creations against ourselves and said nonsense like "I would buy it but it's too big for me" (whilst holding a size eight). Or "I would buy it, but I don't think it goes with any of my shoes", until even we grew tired of the jape.

For six months everywhere we went Pastor Elliot's face beamed down at us, and every time we saw him it would set us off again. This was several years ago, but we still say we liked someone's outfit, but it isn't Pastor Elliot worthy.

Then someone heard us mention Pastor Elliott and knew who we were talking about! her Mum had managed to get tickets to his service, we were understandably excited, and wanted to hear all about it.

Would you believe it? all the effort the congregation had gone to, and he didn't see any of it… because he appeared by video link.

# Childhood friends

I do admire people who keep friendships they made in childhood. They say "oh we met in Mrs So and So's class in infant's school. Or "our parents have always been friends, so we were besties before we were even born". How incredibly lovely and Enid Blyton. Am I jealous? Well maybe a tiny weeny bit.

My old friend candidates consist of Victoria Plum, a girl I spent all my time with at junior school. She had curly hair and an older brother (both things eight year old me longed for), so I thought she was fabulous. We spent every playtime together, sat next to each other in class. And I went to her house for tea too many times to count (for what I believe the young people now call 'play dates'). She was very special to little me.

Her parents had made part of their loft into a play area, and we took a record player up there. Sitting on huge cushions, listening to music and eating sweets under the eaves of the house were some of my happiest times.

The only sticking point was my eating habits, which I am sure they thought were a little basic. An example being my refusal to eat salad, despite their repeated attempts to encourage me. Being a nice family, they felt genuine shock that I would not eat anything on a jacket potato except a ton of butter, and some grated cheese.

There was no way I would eat a salad where all the ingredients were in one bowl. As a sensitive child any food that touched any other food was a no no. A school dinners plate where everything sat in its own compartment would have been great. But in those days, it was not possible to buy them, sensitive kids needed to just "stop being difficult", if they knew what was good for them.

I did not even know half the things in the bowl Victoria Plum's mum had included things like radishes and bell peppers. Which I would not meet and try properly until I was much older. That seemed the height of sophistication to me and went way beyond anything served at my house.

Our salad consisted of a cos lettuce, a tomato, and a stick of celery. Even pickled onions only came out at an official buffet. I cannot swear to it, but the salad I refused to eat may even have had a dressing on it, but I could be making that up.

## Friends Like These

When senior school loomed, I petitioned my parents to be able to go to the same one as Victoria. Which also happened to be a very well performing school academically. However, it meant catching a coach at eight o'clock each morning, which Mum said she wasn't keen on me having to do.

I found out much later that excuse hid a dastardly ulterior motive. Years later mum admitted she thought the headmaster of the terrible school was "really handsome, and just so tall…." And that if I went there, she could spend five years ogling him. Which naturally trumped all other considerations.

Anyway, I didn't know that at the time, and just had to cope with knowing that in September Victoria Plum and I would part ways. Her for an academic girl's school with an impeccable reputation, me for a community comprehensive with a decidedly unsavoury one. And is so often the case we didn't see or speak to each other again once we were in different schools.

Twenty years later my mum met her mum at a thing and remembered that her daughter had been my friend. She asked various questions so that she was able to report back. VP had a grown up job, a husband, and a baby on the way said Mum. So, nothing like me then.

Mum also found out when Victoria would be visiting so she could engineer a reunion. I did wonder whether we would reminisce and rekindle the childhood friendship that had meant so much to me. Or if we would be too different now. Regardless, I thought it would be fun to meet and catch up.

As luck would have it, I didn't have to wait too long to find out, thanks to some complications with her pregnancy VP was off work and visiting her mum more than usual. When we bumped into them in town, mum suggested a coffee for us, and a nibble on a ginger biscuit for her so we could catch up.

The blank look she gave me showed that I didn't appear anywhere in her brain. Not even in the very back of her memory, floating around in the mists of time. Nothing. She had been precious to me, yet she hadn't even remembered my existence. Now that was a kick in the trousers. But it also made me wonder, who was the friend she remembered from primary school?

During the Victoria Plum years I had been friends with another child. Her mum conveniently happened to be friends with my mum. We were at each other's houses every single week, and so it made sense, what else would we do?

## Friends Like These

Unusually, but probably because our mums knew each other, I had been allowed to stay overnight at her house. It had gone well, popcorn in front of a video, and giggling into the night. It was all fine in fact, until breakfast time. When her mum had used an entire pint of full fat milk on three Weetabix, and I hadn't eaten more than a couple of mouthfuls. She had told me off for wasting food and money, then made a formal complaint to my mum. All she had to do was ask me and I would have told her that at home we had one Weetabix with a dribble of milk.

A big breakfast was not a familiar concept, and I would never be able to eat all that first thing in the morning. In the early eighties if someone else's parent told you off then yours would follow up with a punishment of their own for having embarrassed them.

Parents often treated all children as they would their own. No-one seemed to consider for a moment that each family had their own way of doing things, their own rules, and expectations. That a child may be brought up completely differently, never seemed to occur to anyone. They certainly didn't easily accommodate any internal or emotional differences; this was generally seen as being picky or being spoilt but was definitely seen as a nuisance.

Being told off by someone else's parents was an awful feeling. And what made it much worse for me, was that as we never had anyone come home to play, my parents never ever told off any other children. It really didn't seem fair at all.

Anyway, it was many years later, in a lecture on brain development when I vaguely recognised a face. This in itself was unusual for me, as facial recognition has never been part of my skill set.

There was something familiar about this woman, I couldn't place her, but still felt sure I knew her somehow. Looking her up on our courses online forum her first name gave it away – I thought she was milk girl.

It took a while before we were both online at the same time, so that I could ask her if her mum was Mrs Milk Girl, my heart skipped a beat when she confirmed that she was. I braced myself, this could be it, the time I got myself a friend from childhood. "We did enjoy some laughs" I said. And - nothing.

We had slept in the same bed people! and she didn't remember anything about me - NOT A THING! I was obviously a most memorable child.

# Further Education

I cannot remember anything about how the friendship between Rebecca and me started. Just that we were the quiet, nerdy girls in our maths class, and then one day we were best friends.

Although we only shared two classes a week, I was more than happy to miss my own classes so that we could hang out in the refectory. Where we laughed, and drank coffee from a vending machine, how very grown up. We learnt to play poker, talked about the boys we knew (basically no-one), and the boys we wished we knew (everyone else). And we people watched in the library, all of which amounted to not doing any actual work. You can tell what crazy rebellious things we were.

So much of our time was spent avoiding classes, whether hiding in the library, or in one of the canteens. We preferred being anywhere on campus other than where we were supposed to be. School days still loomed large in our minds, and we didn't want to be caught in the wrong place and hauled back into our lesson.

Looking back, we thought we were much more noticeable and important than we ever were. I doubt anyone would have said anything to us, had they even noticed we were not where we were meant to be.

Rebecca was one year and five months older than me, and so although quieter, she was the leader. Besides her age she also had two things I wasn't likely to have anytime soon, namely a driving license, and a car. This enabled us, when we were feeling particularly daring, to leave the campus altogether.

But not having this daredevil thing down pat at all, we only went as far as Rebecca's house. Her mum (who I always remember as being at home) would make us snacks. She did an excellent line in homemade cakes, and expensive chocolate biscuits, which was fine by me.

To my knowledge Mrs Rebecca's Mum never once asked us about appearing in the middle of the day. Never questioned whether we should be studying, or in a lesson. Mine knew where I was supposed to be to the millimetre. It was the time before mobile phones, and phone tracking software. So, my mum had resorted to keeping my college timetable pinned to her kitchen cork board. And every time I appeared she'd refer to the board to make sure I was supposed to be at home before even saying hello.

Sometimes Mrs Rebecca's Mum would say 'auntie so and so saw your car somewhere or other'. Then Rebecca would get all flustered, and either make up something obviously rubbish, about why it hadn't been her car, or a convoluted alternative explanation of where she had been.

Other times she would explode, complaining loudly about always being under surveillance. At those times, her mum would plead "we're just trying to look out for you darling", and a mother daughter heart to heart would begin, with me trapped in its fringes.

Although physically in the room I became able to turn off my ears and would do so at these moments rather than risk dying of pure embarrassment. At sixteen the chances of this felt perilously high.

For me, the best times were when she'd draw me into her story. I was happy to agree with whatever she said. And loved being part of her excuse/alibi. It was fun to be included in a secret, despite not knowing what the secret was. I never asked her to tell me what was going on, it seemed obvious to me if she wanted to tell me what was going on nothing was stopping her. Little did I guess.

In the times we did go to our lectures our tutor took every opportunity to poke fun at us for being joined at the hip, or some such. It was embarrassing, but we just thought he was an idiot. His other entertainment was handing back assignments in order from the highest marks, to lowest. So, everyone knew who was bottom of the class, utterly hilarious (to him at least).

You won't be shocked to hear Rebecca and I always took turns on being second from last, and last. To be fair we never did any studying, so they were our rightful places, but he didn't need to be such a twit about it. We failed every test, and with seemingly no understanding of teenagers, he sent us to another room on our own to retake them. Which left us in peace so we could, and did, try to help each other. Despite our joint efforts we were still bottom of the class.

After repeated warnings from my personal tutor about failing to attend classes, I got expelled from college before the Christmas term was even over. I didn't really care, my mum on the other hand was furious. Rebecca and I began to spend less and less time together. Without our own phones we hardly spoke.

## Friends Like These

It was actually during a meet up with another friend, that a rumour about the maths lecturer and a student was mentioned to me. Naturally I thought it was ridiculous gossip, and can clearly remember saying "but he's old, and he wears socks with sandals". I couldn't imagine anyone would be interested in him. Many people wear this combo now, and no-one bats an eyelid. But then it was the fashion kiss of death.

My friend reported, not only was the gossip in full swing but someone was being suggested as the lecturer's lover. The person in question? you've guessed it haven't you? That's right, he mentioned Rebecca.

"Utterly impossible" I said, "she would never" I said, "they must be mad" I said, "that's just wrong" I said. Of course, it wasn't, she would, they weren't, and it wasn't.

Some weeks later she telephoned me, as she wanted to tell me the news herself, before I heard from anyone else (too late). She said she had been lonely after I left, and had started spending time with him, and it had just sort of developed. They weren't just having an affair; they were in a relationship. So, you could say that it was all my fault really.

As it turned out they had been having an affair the entire time, which was why she was so shady about where her car was seen. Socks and sandals not withstanding they ended up living together, although she always said it wouldn't be a long term thing, that was twenty years ago, and to my knowledge they are still an item.

It's no wonder then that his main worry wasn't about us cheating on our maths tests.

# Radical Restyle

In our early twenties Bliss, Amy, Sal and I moved into a shared house, we had a whale of a time. With every weekend a party, soon all our friends knew each other, and more miraculously got on. Unfortunately, breast and ovarian cancer ran in Bliss's family. And after losing her granny, two aunties, and a cousin, her doctor suggested she had genetic testing.

The tests would show how likely she was to go on to develop either disease herself. Before this, like many twenty somethings, her biggest decisions had been whether to splurge on a new outfit, or where to take a holiday.

Now she found herself having to make lifechanging choices. As inexperienced as we were, we all tried to give her what she needed to get through it. And we really did our best, in our own ways. But all she wanted, when asked, was for us to try and behave as normally as possible (something we struggled with at the best of times).

## Eden Gruger

She didn't want to speak about any of it, refused to in fact. And if anything, partied harder than before, which was saying something. We tried to take her lead, but when she wasn't around it was all we could talk about. We tried to understand what it must be like for her and work out how we were going to support her.

Finally, Bliss called a house meeting, sat us all down, and revealed that not only had she gone ahead with the testing, but she already had the results. She had been given an eighty percent chance of developing both diseases before the age of thirty.

We cried as she explained about being offered a double mastectomy, and hysterectomy. We were devastated for her; this came as a massive blow to her plans for a family. And now she had to weigh up whether her dreams for the future were worth the risk to her life.

It was so hard to comprehend, suddenly she was an adult, and we were lagging way behind her. Amy read about possible treatment options and outcomes. Sal bought her as many cocktails as she demanded.

I went into super practical mode, and checked where she would be having her treatment. A new unit had opened locally, and I would show my care by raising funds for the department Bliss would use.

## Friends Like These

Weeks and various ideas came and went, but nothing felt like it would raise enough money. One by one each plan was rejected. Until that is, the morning I sat up in bed and heard myself say I planned to be sponsored to shave my head. It also meant Bliss wouldn't be the only one losing her hair, I hoped that meant she wouldn't feel quite so alone.

My boyfriend tried to mention how much I liked to change my hairstyle, before choosing to go along with the idea. I think he knew anything else would just be a waste of time. In the spirit of gung-ho I emailed everyone I knew and started planning. As a person with tons of starting energy this stage was an absolute joy to me. Making lists, firing off ideas, contacting people and asking for favours, there was virtually nothing else in my head.

After asking everyone to sponsor me, I asked them to ask everyone *they* knew to sponsor me. Imagine doing all this by actually speaking to people rather than being able to use social media. All of this was a good start but wasn't building the funds as fast as I thought they should be growing. So, when people asked if they could be at the actual head shaving, it became obvious it needed to happen in public. That would definitely get more attention for the cause. Some readers might be shocked to hear we didn't need to consider any health and safety issues. There were no questionnaires, and no-one considered insurance. The whole scheme hung on an idea, and a department store who said we could use their shop front. What daredevils we were! it was definitely a more naive time. No-one ever thought of being sued, and litigation was just a word on American television programmes.

With the venue agreed, and a date chosen, my hairdresser was persuaded to come and do the deed. She waived her fee in exchange for a promise that the first pass of the razer could be down the centre of my head. My parents were looking forward to coming along and rattling collection buckets, you could practically mug someone if you had a charity collection pot then. An entertainer friend agreed to juggle on his unicycle to catch people's eye. And I invited anyone who thought it would be funny to come and watch.

The morning of the shaving, dad and I packed the car with everything we would need. While mum busied herself putting on her ever trusty tinsel wig (she did love a bit of sparkle).

Many people have asked whether I was nervous at this point. But I can honestly say the reality of walking around with a shaved head for months on end hadn't even occurred to me. Ahh the joy and

## Friends Like These

pain of hyperfocus, and having made up my mind to do it, nothing could distract me.

As the cape was swirled around my shoulders, I did feel a little burst of something that could have been anxiety or excitement hard to tell which. But it was easily shaken off, this was what I had worked for, the market stall holders, shoppers and curious onlookers giggling and pointing, wouldn't be enough to stop me now.

My hairdresser ever the retiring sort bellowed for attention, and announced she was about to start shaving my head. As agreed, the first buzz of the razor went straight down the centre of my head. Accompanied by gasps and guffaws from the crowd, four more passes and the deed was done. I was shorn, my head was very white and very chilly. The strands previously known as 'my hair' blew around in the windy market square like busy ginger mice.

Everyone cheered (they really did), and the sounds of coins clattering into the collection tins was deafening. Many people came up to us to speak about their own cancer stories, or to ask if I was mad. It wasn't until after the crowds had gone, my hair had been swept up, and everything had been packed away, that Bliss made her big revelation.

## Eden Gruger

She had decided to take her chances and not go ahead with any of the offered treatments after all. Which was of course her right, but also a bit of a shock given that I was now completely bald.

I have always wondered why she hadn't mentioned this to me before the day, she knew what I was doing and why. And have concluded that she was just a really private person. What other explanation could there be? On the plus side I managed to raise twelve hundred pounds. Which to put it in context was half the cost of a basic kitchen around that same time.

It didn't take long for my new look to be embarrassing. Reactions varied between strange looks, people sniggering, or whispering behind their hands not very subtly. If my Mum was with me, it got much worse, as she would jump in and say that I had my head shaved for charity. Many of those people donated money right then. Whether to relieve the embarrassment of having misjudged me, or to get mum to leave them alone, we'll never know. The almost constant "you are brave I couldn't do that", comments did get a bit much.

A week later an amazingly unflattering picture of me appeared on the front page of the local newspaper. Yes, there was a paper edition of local news. It included photographs of local houses for sale, and often several pages of job adverts. The headline proclaimed, 'local woman shaves head', over a picture of my newly shaved scalp shyly reflecting the daylight. The photographer had got me to balance my hair in the palm of my hand and puff my cheeks out as if blowing the hair away. It could not have been less flattering.

Not only was the photo embarrassing, but it was the first time anyone had ever referred to me as a woman. Before that moment I had always thought of myself as a slip of a girl, and I can clearly remember the indignation. It took almost as long for me to recover from that, as it did for my hair to grow back.

Over the following months, my peanut head (because that was roughly what shape it turned out to be). Evolved into a hedgehog, with spikes of hair sticking in all directions. Not fetching on anyone other than Dennis the Menace.

What I would say is that it was nice to see my real hair colour (for a bit anyway).

# Cold Soup and Amphibians

I had planned to explain my friendship with Charlotte by saying we all need one person in our life who is willing to push themself outside their comfort zone. Particularly when it's in hopes of winning a bet.

Then I realised that not everybody will have been as lucky as me, there aren't many Charlottes, and some very mature people might not want a friend who is up for anything. That's a pity, because a Charlotte type can be relied upon to make you laugh and challenge your sense of shame. Quite a hefty combination in one person.

Don't think she doesn't feel embarrassment, that she is shameless, because she does, and she isn't. It's just that being entertaining, and spending any winnings her bets bring in, are quite enough to ease any pain she might feel.

## Friends Like These

I met my Charlotte, while working in a very small department of an extremely large organisation. It alternated between being incredibly busy, and completely inactive. This gave us plenty of time to bond (our colleagues all thought we were nuts), over our shared horror of the smell of cold soup, discovered one day in the staff kitchen. And an extreme distrust of amphibians. And yes, it's perfectly possible to build a friendship on those grounds, Ms Judgy Pants.

Any time we spent together even when work was hectic, was full of the nonsensical, and we often laughed until our stomachs ached. One hot summers afternoon Charlotte came with me to pick the boyfriend up from work. My concept of time being a little wobbly to say the least, I was normally late for everything. However, in an effort not to leave him standing out in the roasting sun, this time we had left far too early. And had enough time to buy a lolly and eat it sat on the bonnet of my car. Many grown ups would say don't do that, it's not good for the bodywork, but I say pah! it's what cool kids do.

We had that let out of school early feeling of being young and carefree as we ate our lollies and tried not to make eye contact with passers-by. If there is a way to eat an ice lolly that isn't obscene, I have yet to find it. Charlotte noticed a road sweeper, an actual man with a uniform and a cart complete with a range of brooms.

Where we lived a little motorised cart with a set of whirling brushes went along the gutters. In our state of semi heat stroke and sugar rush we thought this man most entertaining.

We watched as he went into various shops, and commented on how trusting he was, I mean anything might happen. Someone could steal his brooms, yes, someone could steal them, couldn't they?

The idea might not have grabbed us quite so much if it weren't for the heat, and the sugar overload. Sadly, we were quite delirious by this point, and even the idea gave us the giggles.

What else could I have done, but challenge her to steal the whole trolley? Still having some of her lollipop left put her off. Then I added the ultimate lure, that if she managed it (without getting caught) she'd earn herself twenty quid.

Charlotte swallowed the last bite of her lolly, shoved the stick into her pocket and was off the bonnet in a moment. Gasping she heaved the cart around the corner, later admitting it had been much heavier than she had expected.

## Friends Like These

After a few seconds she strolled casually towards the car while I howled with laughter. Like the immature twits we were, we felt the need to hide, while we waited for the road sweeper to come back to the spot he expected his stuff to be in. We chose to hunker down in the passenger footwells.

We didn't need to wait long; the sweeper approached the empty spot where his trolley should be and threw his arms into the air. We exploded, he stomped around the corner, and then reappeared with the cart before carrying on along the street. He didn't even bother to look around for the culprit.

At this point my boyfriend opened the backdoor and slid onto the seat. Shaking his head, he said, "we heard you cackling hyenas from upstairs," and set us off again by saying "poor bloke, people are always hiding his cart".

It may not have been original, but it was still flipping funny, and yes. I did give her the promised twenty.

# What is this thing I hear you speak of?

Some of you may not understand what you are about to read. If you are one of those people, I presume you are neurotypical. Partial congrats, you more than likely understand most of the social rules, and what the heck other people are on about. If you are wondering why I'm not congratulating you whole heartedly, it's because I think you are missing out on some wicked brain adaptions, but we won't go into that here.

What I am about to share might not make sense the first time around. If it doesn't, I suggest you grab a cuppa, and have another go. It will give you some idea about what life feels like for those of us whose brains do things differently. You'll find some good stuff here to help you understand some of the many ways us divergent brained people differ from you in the everyday world.

## Friends Like These

It's all thanks to an interesting therapist I had who perfectly understood my love of lists and spreadsheets, that I can share this with you now. She knew that making a chart would help me understand the idea of friendship.

So there now exists a timeline stretching over ten years which shows my journey from seeing friendships on television and thinking 'well that looks interesting'. Through to actually developing and maintaining some of my own.

In another life I would probably be a research scientist so strong is my love of collating data. I know that I am not alone, after all isn't that why people write journals and diaries? Because it's interesting to look back and see how life has progressed.

As I said television and how people in it behaved was part of how I saw relationships. But books were the real influencer, the Enid Blyton and Arthur Ransome friendships where people were part of each other's adventures, could give each other a dose of honest advice if someone was being daft. But were always there in each other's hour of need. You could make a great friend in an instant, simply by sharing your cola bottles or something similar. And that was you set for life, but as you will know that isn't quite how things work in the world.

Eden Gruger

The spreadsheet was saved under the heading 'How Friendship Works' (don't you just love a needlessly dramatic title?). With columns for acquaintances, mates, friends, and best friends. Should you make your own list you can make your own categories of course, but these were mine.

Seeing it written down really helped me begin to understand the boundaries of these relationships. You probably take for granted the social rules, but trust me when I say people do not like it one little bit if you muddle them and 'how things work'.

Let's get the ball rolling with acquaintances, after all this is roughly where all relationships start. This could be someone you have met in real life or online. Your knowledge of these people could range from knowing a little, or quite abit depending on how forthcoming they are, or how much alcohol has been involved in your meeting.

The main characteristic I have found in these people is that when you ask how they are, they usually say "fine". And that is the answer they are hoping for when they ask you. It was quite frustrating to find that someone would ask how you are but didn't want an honest answer.

How nonsensical! why flipping ask?

## Friends Like These

I did have a habit before having my categories of giving too much of myself to people in this group and being disappointed when they disappeared. Now I understand these people are not friends, they are one step up from strangers really.

You may see them several times in quick succession, or hardly ever, with years in between. It can be in relation to an activity or a larger group.

The idea is to not tell them anything much that goes on in your life, and you shouldn't massively care if anything happened to them. If you heard they had been trampled by an elephant, say, you would be interested. But mainly because they would probably be the first person you know to be killed by a pachyderm, but they wouldn't be leaving a gaping hole in your life.

These are also the people who it is socially acceptable to blatantly lie to, this continues to stump me. People often say, "we must do something", or "let's get together", but don't you believe a word of it! they don't mean it at all. Why on earth would you say something you don't mean? I mean why would you though?

The answer apparently is because it is manners to make people think you like them more than you do, by pretending you want to spent time with them when you don't. Kind, eh? nope not in my brain, offering something you have no intention of following through with is rude, and hurts people. If you don't want to meet someone or do something with them, say nothing, try it, you'll find it saves loads of energy.

Anyway, back to the next level, Mates, you find out you have something in common with an acquaintance, you start to see them more, or contact them. And you are likely to get some joint social activities at this level.

You may both choose to share personal information, this is the getting to know you stage of human relationships, and it may develop into something more, or might not. It is quite a fun phase; no-one is supposed to be asking too much of anyone and it's mainly enjoyable.

I have to mention where you are most likely to get tripped up at this stage. Some people will ask you to help them, which you would do because after all you are a lovely person aren't you? But once you have finished doing the things they wanted, whether that be mending their bike, icing cakes with their child, looking after their cat, seeing them through a breakup. A need to borrow £200 for Christmas presents.

## Friends Like These

You stop hearing from them and they move on.

This has happened to me more times than you can shake a stick at (what an odd saying). This does not necessarily mean the askers are bad people, or are leading you on, although some of them definitely are both. Also, if they are really great then they will have actual friends to do these things for them, and with them. All I am saying is watch yourself.

It is also important to note that some relationships stay at this level forever. They never develop, which is fine, and someone can be a fabulous mate, who you have loads of fun with, as and when. Just don't try calling them in the middle of the night to take you to hospital because your arm is hanging off. If this keeps happening to you, does it mean you struggle with getting close to people? Not necessarily it might just show you are being discerning.

Make it through the first two rounds, and things might develop on both sides enough to be at the Friends level. Here you get the social activities, the reciprocal revelation *and* wait for it, because it's a long time coming, mutual support. You know real stuff about them, and you call each other in a crisis real, or imagined. It's probable that your values align, and you are at a similar stage in life. Welcome, this is friendship.

Eden Gruger

Apparently, the average adult has three close friends, which sounds like a healthy number. What we cannot be sure about is if that is three separate friendships, or one foursome. It sounds like an awful lot of work to have three separate lots of everything to remember.

Even now you need to keep your wits about you, to make sure this stays a two way arrangement. Set the limits of time and energy that you are comfortable with giving, and make sure you respect the other persons boundaries too. Get it wrong at this point and you could find yourself bumped off their chart altogether.

Friendship can be very beautiful and long lasting, or beautiful and not for long. You must have heard that for a season or for a reason thing. It might be encouraged into existence by your children being in the same class, you work in the same place. Or you are both going through a divorce or learning a skill. Change one of these factors, and you are out of sync, and cannot quite bring it back into place. It can still be great while it lasted.

Three years ago, my friend block had six names, today as I write it now has two. It turned out that three of the originals had been acquaintances, and one a mate. They included a person who I lodged with, who needed help to renovate her shop. A month after the relaunch party, that I organised, they increased the rent on my room, and I could no longer afford it. And the one who planned a craft project and needed me to cut out hundreds of bits of paper. Who once the work was done mysteriously always seemed to be busy when I called.

But that's ok, because I was just learning how things worked then.

# Sounds So Fake It Must Be True

There are sometimes in life when the real reason for being late sounds like the worse kind of made-up, nonsensical bull crap. And this was definitely one of those times. As if working a full time job during the day wasn't enough, Sammie decided to take an on-call security job three nights a week.

Not because she loved working so much, or because she didn't want any time off. It was to help her save towards a mortgage deposit (or to go travelling, she constantly changed her mind over which was her main priority). But when she did choose, she wanted to be prepared.

Fortunately, job number two was mainly a sleeping night shift, so after doing a check of the building, she was allowed to sleep unless, and until there was an emergency. The company provided a little bedroom that had previously been a cupboard (so no windows) with a bed, radio, TV, sink and tea making facilities for the person to hang out in.

They didn't provide anywhere to shower as the person had to stay in uniform, in case of the previously mentioned emergency. On the wall next to the bed was a large switchboard of buzzers and lights to wake her up and show her where she was needed.

Around mid morning on the day of her first shift Sammie realised her phone had been suspiciously quiet. And on closer inspection noticed it was turning itself on and off. Now, technology may be clever, and often works in mysterious ways, but she knew that wasn't right.

This was more of a disaster than you might think, given that the address of her new job was tucked away in the phone. She didn't know it having been interviewed by an agency off site. All she could remember was that it was a twenty minute cycle between her office and the evening job. Here she was with only a few hours until her new job started, and she had no idea where it was, their contact details or the supervisor's name. The rest of the morning passed in a blur of stress and overthinking.

As the phone needed more attention than Sammie could give it, she rushed straight to the phone shop during her lunch break. Where the helpful assistant pressed the on off button a few times, attempted to charge the phone beyond the 100% it already showed, and then confirmed that the phone was, in fact broken.

Sammie bought the second to cheapest option available. Before grabbing lunch and running back to the office, stressed, red, and more than a little sweaty.

It was about two hours later when checking on the phone which was charging under the desk, Sammie found that it didn't work with her sim card. So, she still had an utterly useless phone. Would she make it back to the shop in time? what if a meeting overran? what if the phone shop closed on time? or worse, a bit early? Luckily, none of these predictions came true, and Sammie managed to get back to the phone shop with a few minutes to spare before they closed for the night.

As it was the assistant's mistake getting the phone refunded and exchanged went without any hiccups. Now all Sammie had to do was find somewhere to charge the phone enough to access the address of where she needed to be.

She slipped into a nearby pub and plugged the phone in, then nipped into the ladies to change into her uniform. With the minimum charge needed to fire up

## Friends Like These

the new phone and use its map system, she was off. Adrenalin pumping, she popped the phone into its cradle on her bicycle handlebars and set off.

She was so delighted with herself, that she decided she could afford a couple of minutes to work on her midlife crisis plan. Riding her bike with no hands was the first step that she hoped to master. In case she wanted to become a trick cyclist, and runaway to join the circus. My friends are what you would call a 'colourful' bunch.

Builders on a nearby scaffold whistled and cheered as she cycled past with her hands on her head. The cat that ran across the road had no idea about Sammie's potential circus plan. So, it couldn't have guessed that her hands were not on the handlebars, and no-where near the brakes.

Managing to miss the cat by millimetres, she wobbled wildly, her balance not expecting to be so suddenly tested. Sammie grabbed at the brakes, squeezing them so hard that the front wheel locked. Sending her somersaulting over the handlebar in quite an acrobatic manoeuvre, most ironic considering her circus plans.

Seeing their entertainment end with such a dramatic flourish, a couple of the builders came down from the scaffold to check on her. Which was nice of them wasn't it? they checked her over, and made sure that Sammie hadn't banged her head, while she did her best to convince them that she was fine to leave without first aid.

Being helped up out of the road by the men who had been applauding her only seconds before, was excruciating. But nowhere near as bad as arriving at a new job nearly fifteen minutes late.

She limped into reception, wheeling a bicycle with a buckled front tyre. Sporting grazes on her cheek, and the palms of both hands. The receptionist ran to help, assuming that she had been the victim of a hit and run. Until Sammie interrupted her commiserations and admitted the truth.

Thankfully the manager was a pragmatic sort of chap, and just shrugged and said, "that sounds so fake, it must be true". The grazes were all healed, the bike was back from the repair shop. And another new phone had replaced the previous new one that had its screen smashed in the accident, by the time we were told the story.

We gasped, shook our heads and laughed in all the right places, all except for Louise that is. She just sat there looking dreamy, until saying breathily "How romantic…" Sammie shook her head, but before I could ask what on earth she was on about, she continued. "Imagine if you ended up married to one of those builders, explaining to your children that their dad jumped off some scaffolding to rescue you".

We love her, we really do, but she is such a silly cow.

# When sharing is bad for you

When my elderly aunt Mabel died, she left me an inheritance, which although not tons of money was enough to boost my wages and help me rent a house.

I searched for something that would be affordable after Mabel's gift ran out. And managed to find a tiny cottage in a lovely village, with a quaint green opposite. It was everything I had wished for, including that Robert the lovely landlord didn't mind me bringing Basa (my old rescue cat) with me.

With help from a friend, we were in and getting settled within a month. I was delighted that she only lived a short distance away in the next village along. Although not able to drive, she didn't mind the walk, so we were able to see each other a few times a week after I had finished work. Sometimes I collected her and took her to the nearest town to look at the shops (not that either of us could actually afford to buy anything), or for a coffee.

She would often telephone me while I was on my lunch break, but on one particular day the conversation felt weird. She was distracted and not her usual self at all. And let slip that she hadn't been out of bed for long and had been dizzy and sick when she woke up.

I laughed and asked if she was pregnant, she laughed too, until she started to work out the dates of her last period. The line went quiet as she realised she was two weeks late.

My break over we ended the call, but she promised to get a test that afternoon. Needless to say at 5:32pm my phone rang with the news she was pregnant.

It was always quite exciting having a pregnant friend, as it allowed me to join in the fun bits, without any of the stretch marks, constipation or of course, having to give birth.

Unfortunately, this time all day morning sickness drained all the excitement out of the situation, as well as all the energy out of my poor friend.

At twelve weeks she felt ok enough to venture out with me for the first time. As it was a warm spring afternoon, we strolled arm in arm under the blossom trees. It was after we had wandered in companionable silence for a bit that she suddenly said, "he pushed me".

It was such a shock; I had never seen any of those kinds of comments that make an outsider wince. Nothing to make me concerned, but as my mum always said it's only the two people in the relationship who really know it.

I hugged her tight while she told me how she wanted to leave but couldn't. I offered to help her find somewhere, but she didn't want to run and hide she said. She would only be able to leave him if she had a way to make a home for her and the baby. One where she didn't need to rely on him for anything. And that had to start with getting out of their village to somewhere she could find work within walking distance.

Seeing her so sad and in such need of safety, the answer seemed obvious, and I knew exactly what to do. Without a moment's hesitation I offered to lend her half of my rent nest egg as a deposit for a flat in town.

Crying with relief she thanked me, she would be ok, with my help she would make a safe life for her and her baby.

Friends Like These

Taking my bank details so that she could set up a standing order to start paying me back a few pounds each month. We parted company that afternoon with a hug, and a promise that I would transfer the money the following day so she could start looking for flats straight away.

Days went passed as I waited to hear from her about when she was leaving, her plans, anything at all. When I messaged her there was no reply, it began to worry me that something had gone seriously wrong when she told him she was leaving. I felt that I had no choice but to visit in person to find out what was happening.

There was no reply when I knocked on the door, which wasn't reassuring. I tried ringing her phone from the doorstep, it went to voicemail.

While I was dithering on the path wondering what to do, her neighbour came out. Luckily, she recognised me and told me my friend had gone to hospital earlier in the day because she had started to bleed. It was dreadful news, I put a note through the letterbox telling her I had popped around and was thinking about her.

A couple of days later when her name flashed up on my phone, I answered to hear wracking sobs.

Sadly, she had lost the baby, and asked me to visit her. Within an hour I was there, holding her hand and listening as she talked it out. It was every bit as harrowing as you might expect.

Her partner, who also looked distraught, brought in a pot of tea then left the room. After a few hours she had talked herself out and cried herself to sleep. Carefully tucking a blanket around her, I crept out.

Although we messaged each other every day she told me she didn't feel up to having visitors. As the weeks passed into months, I wanted to ask her how things were going with her partner, if she was still leaving, but it never seemed like the right time. It was probably about four months later when I eventually suggested popping around after work, and to my surprise, and relief, she agreed.

The woman who opened the door was quite a different one from the one whose sleeping body I had tucked up all those weeks earlier. She gave me a big smile, grabbed my hand and pulled me inside. It was good although unexpected considering her recent mood, to see her like this.

I wasn't sure what to do, she had gone through some awful things. A relationship gone toxic, an unexpected pregnancy, and then it's loss. And had been messaging about her sadness, anger, maybe even depression. Yet now, here she was practically dancing in front of me.

By the time we sat down with a coffee I just had to ask what was going on? how things were with her partner? was she still planning to leave? She looked confused and shook her head, "Leave? Why would I leave?"

She looked at me as if I had said something quite ridiculous, and said she was hardly likely to leave when she'd just had the bedroom decorated – they had even had a proper carpenter in to build some fitted wardrobes.

The floor felt like it was tipping away from me as I said, "but what about the money I lent you for somewhere safe to live?" She looked me straight in the eye when she said, "it's not your business what I do with my money."

Still sitting on her sofa, I logged into my online bank, only one payment had ever been made, on the first month I loaned her the money. To say I was shellshocked would be an understatement. We had spoken to each other more than a hundred times since then, and she had never said a word.

Eden Gruger

I asked, "What happened to paying me back each month?", she said she didn't know anything about any payments! and as far as she was concerned the money had been a gift.

I left her house shaking and went home in utter disbelief. Had he found the money and taken it? had she been brainwashed? How would I cover my own bills comfortably in the months to come now that Auntie Mabel's money was never coming back?

Over the coming sleepless nights, I struggled to believe this person who I had been so close to could do this. My efforts to speak to her, text and write to her were all ignored.

In fact, I never saw or spoke to her again. I found out over the following year, that there was a long line of people from previous friends to landlords that this person owed money to.

When I visited the County court to ask their advice they knew her by name, which I think says a lot.

# Strawberry Cervix

My friend who asked not to remain nameless (Ok Jay?) had booked her cervical smear test for just after work. The hope being that the business of the day would distract her from having her hoo ha looked at in a medical way.

What really happened was that despite being rushed off her feet, she had put up with low level anxiety ticking away in the back of her mind all day. What is it about a stranger putting a metal instrument up your parts that is so unnerving? Having said that, I know some people like this kind of thing, which is totally fine for them (no judgement here).

Jay arrived a few minutes before her appointment, she had planned to nip to the ladies, and give herself a thorough once over with a wet wipe. Not environmentally friendly, but easy to hide in a handbag.

Unfortunately, as soon as she walked in, she saw the nurse chatting in reception. Before the automatic door even had time to swish closed, the nurse had asked her name, and said "come on through, let's get you in and out".

Like a lot of us when flustered Jay could not think straight. So didn't even think to say she needed to go to the ladies and buy herself some tidying up time. Instead, she allowed herself and her day warm lady area to be ushered into the surgery.

Mortified she plonked into a chair while they ran through the obligatory pre-smear test questions, no, she couldn't be pregnant, her last period started fourteen days ago. No, she wasn't on oral contraceptives. Yes, she would use barrier methods of birth control should she ever have sex. No, she had no pain, weird discharge, or unexplained symptoms.

This done the nurse asked Jay to take her bottom off, (now this kind of thing always appeals to me, it is abit like someone asking me to put the kettle on. My immature / pedantic response is usually my bottom doesn't come off, and I wouldn't fit into the kettle. Just me then? oh ok).

While wrestling with her tights Jay leaned against the plastic bed only to discover it was roughly the same temperature as the wintery pavement outside. There was just a thin slice of paper couch roll between her buttocks and frostbite. When she told me later, we had quite a chat around whether it would be possible to get chilblains of the anus.

The creak of the bed let the nurse know that Jay was on board. One of her hands swished back the curtain, while the other hand slid the giant spotlight over Jay's nether regions.

Squeezing a large splodge of lubricant onto the speculum, the nurse said, "pop your arms down by your sides, it'll help you relax." Before slipping the duck bill into Jay.

It was while winding the instrument open and reaching for the long swab, that the nurse asked Jay if she planned to have any children. Currently single and undecided Jay said she "hadn't found the right person yet".

"Oh, you don't need to wait for a partner" said the nurse, "you can always pick someone, have their kid then say thanks bye".

While Jay was reeling from the moral implications of this advice, the nurse went on, "you've got a nice healthy looking cervix. You should see some of the things I have to deal with. One woman had one like a strawberry, and when the swab touched her, whoosh it was like strawberry jam everywhere".

With this graphic and scarring insight into the life of a nurse, (which she could've gone without), the nurse withdrew the instrument. Handed Jay some couch roll to wipe the lubricant off herself and disappeared back through the veil of curtains. Leaving Jay both complimented, and shellshocked.

While typing up her notes the nurse said, "I'm glad you were early, I wanted to leave for the pub before there was too much catching up to do".

It was only as she picked her bag up from under the chair, that Jay was at the right angle to spy the pregnant belly pressing against the desk.

# Hula Girl

We were at a festival and had drunk quite a lot of alcohol, which was why we were still up and wandering around in the middle of the night. Talking a mixture of deep insights and nonsense to random people. This was one of the things I loved about going to festivals and events. The normal rules including those of time (a man-made construct anyhoo), went out the window.

We wandered into a big top that was used for an after hours cabaret. Despite the official show ending a couple of hours before there were still a few people sitting around. Someone was juggling very slowly with balloons, there were a couple of unicyclists weaving their way through the almost as wobbly drunks, and in front of the stage there was a woman hula hooping.

We watched and clapped as the hoop rolled from her waist to her shoulders, was lifted above her head. Then dropped down to her knees and back up to her waist. She was lithe and graceful, and seemed oblivious to the people watching. It was 3:24am and I had just met the woman who would become my all-time platonic girl crush.

"You should ask her to teach you" someone said. I shook my head; I couldn't speak to this woman! her confidence and ease intimidated me. But another friend agreed and poked at me (and yes, they did physically poke me) until laughing I gave in and went over. The hooper graciously accepted the compliment that we all thought she was amazing. And smiling said "you could definitely do it" and asked if I wanted to learn.

She rolled a spare hoop towards me, and my first ever hula lesson began. Within minutes she had me moving smoothly, which was quite a feat for a tipsy woman in the early hours of the morning. We laughed together as my ability to keep the ring around my waist and off the floor grew.

Eventually the night moved closer to dawn, and everyone headed back to their tents for some sleep. It was only as I dropped off, I realised I hadn't thought to ask the hoopers name and hadn't heard anyone else use it.

Emerging through the tent flaps after my lay in the following day, a familiar figure strolled across the field to the shower block...it was Hula Girl! I shouted and waved (because I had no understanding of being cool). She smiled, waved back with equal friendliness and carried on her way. We didn't see each other again, and all too soon it was time to go home to normal life.

Two months later I had wrestled my tent up in yet another festival field, and was in the bar. Having learnt the hard way that hitting the bar first, often meant having to sleep in the car. I was still savouring my first pint when who should appear? Hula Girl and a cuddly bear, that I would later discover was her husband.

My delight was tinged with nerves, how would it feel when she didn't recognise me? So, what a joy it was when she caught sight of me and screamed "Hula Girl!" and ran to give me a hug. We spent alot of time together over the next few days, she taught me my first trick (taking the hoop up from waist to neck) which looks very snazzy. We developed in-jokes, and it was she who I was with when I got hit in the head with a frisbee.

We bumped into each other at other festivals that year and the one after and began to meet in 'real life' too. I was delighted when Hula Girl came all the way from Brighton to London for the night to be at my birthday party. The photographs still make me laugh out loud and make my insides all fuzzy.

When hula girl and her husband moved to Yorkshire it wasn't long before I jumped on the train for a visit. Passers-by probably thought we hadn't seen each other in years from the way we ran across the car park shrieking, with arms wide open for a hug. But a better welcome to Yorkshire or anywhere for that matter, I do not know.

Recently, I had a card from her with two very old women hooping. I knew straight away which one of them was me. One definitely looked much less co-ordinated, with her hands at odd angles that made them look really long.

Most ad hoc pictures of me make me look like I'm wearing a giant foam hand, or am ET phoning home. My hands which are naturally long and thin (what they used to call pianists fingers) seem magnified whenever a camera is nearby. Just one of the things that put me off my potential career as a famous supermodel. Seriously you do not want hands like these catching on as the next 'big thing'.

As I write this Hula Girl is now a full grown up with a little person and a house. We don't meet up nearly as much as we did. But no book about friends would be complete without her. I love her, I mean I genuinely do. How we met, how poised and beautiful she is, and how much she loves pick and mix.

I hope that you have enjoyed reading Friends like these, and that it has left you wanting more, and if it has why not check out my other collections.

*Down With Frogs* is a collection of laugh out loud, hilarious, candid, occasionally tragic tales. It has always been said Princesses have to kiss a lot frogs before they find their Prince... so it makes sense that sometimes they might feel like giving up on love. From awkward first meetings, dreadful dinners, to who should do the dusting, and sexual mishaps, dating is a minefield. The big question is will we learn from our mistakes or make them all over again? Whether you are happily settled, or still looking, these laugh out loud, always candid, occasionally tragic tales will delight you.

*Laughing at Myself* – These laugh out loud, hilarious, candid tales of awkward meetings, terrible driving tests, dodgy hairdos and accidentally flashing, show just what a minefield life can be.

The big question is how will we survive the embarrassment?

Whether you are the sort of person who trips over fresh air, or you have the poise of a Queen, these tales will delight you.

You can follow me on social media, and subscribe to my Very Important Readers:

https://edengruger.com/eden-gruger-author

https://www.facebook.com/EdenGrugerTheAuthor

https://www.goodreads.com/author/show/18385919.Eden_Gruger


And don't forget I would really appreciate your leaving a review for this book!

https://edengruger.com/books https://www.amazon.co.uk/Eden-Gruger/e/ B093T6VHCV?

https://www.goodreads.com/author/show/18385919.Eden_Gruger

*Funny Bird* shares some more of the darkly comic stories that make you laugh and cringe in equal measure. This mini collection for my Very Important Readers Group includes The Taxi Driver, Deafness and Accents, He is not Father Dougal and Chip pans and Louvre doors.

Get your free copy when you become a Very Important Reader

https:// subscribepage.io/y9H8Qn

www.ingramcontent.com/pod-product-compliance
Lightning Source LLC
Chambersburg PA
CBHW071032080526
44587CB00015B/2585